EMOTIONS

For inquiries and more information visit www.drkayabeid.com

For Anthony Jr. and Sarai —

I dedicate this book to you, my little loves, as a testament to the incredible power of experiencing your emotions and the gift of self-healing that resides within your heart. You are beacons of love and resilience, and may you always embrace your authentic selves, honoring and following your inner compass, allowing your hearts to sing with joy.

Love, Mama!

In the world of emotions, let's take a ride,
Feel them in your body, let them be your guide.
First, there's happiness, like sunshine on your face,
It sparkles and it dances, all over the place.
With toys and games, and when you're outside,
Mom and dad's warm hugs make happiness reside.
It helps your body stay strong, heal, and grow,
Let happiness inside, let your spirit glow.

Next, meet sadness, a friend who sometimes appears,
When joy takes a break, and there might be tears.
It's in your heart and tummy, it doesn't feel great,
But sadness helps your body process, don't hate.
It's okay to be sad when things don't go your way,
Let it out, let it go, and you'll find a brighter day.

Sometimes frustration makes you feel really mad,
You might scream, yell, and get fiery, oh so bad.
Your voice is loud, your head feels like a weight,
Anger can upset your tummy, it's not great.
But remember, anger is a guest, not here to stay,
Release it in a safe place, in your own way.
Step aside, find your space, let the feelings unfurl,
Stomp your feet, punch pillows, or give a loud whirl.

When fear creeps in, you might feel afraid,
Your belly's all yucky, your body's in the shade.
Shaky hands, racing heart, a monster's charade,
But remember, fear's okay; it keeps you safe, it's your aid.

Worries can be like clouds, darkening your day,
Thoughts that won't leave, making you sway.
Toss and turn, stomach churn, and can't sit still,
Worries help you prepare, give you strength and skill.

Now, find calmness, like a gentle stream's flow,
Relaxed body, peaceful mind, take it slow.
Deep breaths in and out, like a gentle breeze,
Safety all around, put your mind at ease.
It's a cozy blanket, a warm, loving embrace,
In this tranquil state, you'll find your happy place.

Be brave, my dear, when challenges arise,
Stand tall, take a breath, reach for the skies.
Bravery's not the absence of fear, it's the fight,
Finding strength within, shining your light.

Emotions are feathers, colorful and bright,
They flutter and they soar, like a kite in flight.
Happy, sad, mad, afraid, safe, and strong,
They make you uniquely you, where you belong.
It's okay to feel them, it's part of the plan,
Embrace your emotions, be a true-hearted fan.
As you grow and learn, more wisdom you'll glean,
Handling your feelings in ways that are serene.

When you need a hand, someone to understand,
Turn to those you trust, lend a listening hand.
Parents, teachers, friends, they'll be your guide,
In this grand adventure of growing, side by side.
So, my young friend, remember this each day,
Release your emotions in a healthy way.
In this journey of life, as you grow and sup,
Embrace every feeling, and never give up!

www.ingramcontent.com/pod-product-compliance
Ingram Content Group UK Ltd.
Pitfield, Milton Keynes, MK11 3LW, UK
UKHW060123300726
14090UKWH00002B/330

* 9 7 9 8 2 1 8 2 9 0 7 6 4 *